"from mind to mind":
ROBERT BROWNING
AND
J. R. R. TOLKIEN

Chris Walsh

Professor of English Literature
and
Dean of Humanities

An Inaugural Lecture
Delivered at the University of Chester
on 1 December 2005

Chester Academic Press

First published 2007
by Chester Academic Press
Corporate Communications
University of Chester
Parkgate Road
Chester CH1 4BJ

Printed and bound in the UK by the
Learning Resources Print Unit
University of Chester
Cover designed by the
Learning Resources Graphics Team
University of Chester

© Chris Walsh, 2007

All Rights Reserved
No part of this publication may be reproduced, stored in a retrieval system or transmitted in any form or by any means without the prior permission of the copyright owner, other than as permitted by current UK legislation or under the terms of a recognised copyright licensing scheme

A catalogue record for this publication is available from the British Library

ISBN 978-1-905929-40-5

"from mind to mind":
ROBERT BROWNING AND
J. R. R. TOLKIEN

Browning and Tolkien: Worlds apart?

Robert Browning and John Ronald Reuel Tolkien make an unlikely pair. The differences are many and the similarities are not immediately obvious. Browning was born in Camberwell in 1812, and died in Venice in 1889; Tolkien was born in Bloemfontein in 1892, and died in Bournemouth in 1973. Browning was a Londoner who lived for fifteen years in Florence; Tolkien grew up in the Midlands and spent most of his life in Oxford, rarely venturing abroad. Browning was educated at home, immersed in his father's 6,000-volume library, before briefly attending the new University of London; Tolkien was educated at King Edward's School (Birmingham), and at the University of Oxford. Browning's only profession was that of poet; Tolkien worked on the *Oxford English Dictionary*, but thereafter was an academic: at Oxford he was Rawlinson and Bosworth Professor of Anglo-Saxon, then Merton Professor of English Language and Literature. Browning was the great Victorian dramatic poet. Tolkien is best known as the author of the "heroic romance" *The Lord of the Rings,* perhaps the most read book in the twentieth century after the Bible. Browning's dramatic monologues led to the realist novel and modernist poetry; Tolkien was anti-modernist but his writings, while using realist techniques, set the agenda for modern fantasy. Browning never experienced war; Tolkien served in the Lancashire Fusiliers in the First World War and saw action in the Battle of the Somme. Browning had been brought up a Nonconformist, but (after reading Shelley) was briefly an atheist in adolescence, before shaping a religious position somewhere between theism and orthodox Christianity. Tolkien had been received into the Roman Catholic Church as a young boy on his mother's conversion, and remained a devout Catholic all his life. Browning's politics were liberal. Tolkien's inclinations were conservative, though he defined his politics as anarchist.[1] Browning was an ardent admirer of the Italian Renaissance. Tolkien identified passionately with the Northern spirit of the early Middle Ages. ("I desired dragons with a profound desire", he confessed.[2])

Temperamentally they were different, too. Although the view of Browning as incorrigibly optimistic is misleading, there is no denying his ebullience and his robustly positive outlook. By contrast, Tolkien, though like Browning clubbable and much given to laughter, had a deep vein of melancholy, even pessimism – hardly surprising in someone who had lost his parents while a boy, and most of his closest friends in the First World War.

Tolkien's literary interests centred on Old English, Old Icelandic and medieval literature; by the time of Chaucer English literature, in Tolkien's view, had not only passed its chronological halfway point but was also qualitatively in decline. He had no interest in Browning's poetry, and admitted to loathing "The Pied Piper of Hamelin".[3]

Surface differences, however, can sometimes conceal a deeper consonance. Consider their respective religious beliefs. Browning, it is true, penned sharply satirical portraits of Catholic clerics: Renaissance or Victorian,

---

[1] *Letters of J. R. R. Tolkien: A Selection*, ed. by Humphrey Carpenter with Christopher Tolkien (London: Allen & Unwin, 1981), pp. 63-64.
[2] J. R. R. Tolkien, "On Fairy-Stories", in *Tree and Leaf*, new edn (London: HarperCollins, 2001), p. 41.
[3] *Letters of J. R. R. Tolkien*, p. 311.

Italian or English, they hardly get a good press. But you do not have to be a subtle reader of Browning to detect an undercurrent of fascination with Catholicism. After all, his Bishop Blougram, we are told, did say "true things" though he "called them by wrong names".[4]

Why Browning and Tolkien?

But why juxtapose *these* two writers? Well, even modest advances in knowledge and understanding are gained by forging links, and discovering similarities and differences. And the study of literature is, in essence, comparative. Thirty or so years ago it was commonplace for examiners to require students to "compare and contrast" one author or text with another. Now it is curious that while there are thousands of single author studies, and even more general surveys, studies of paired writers are relatively rare. Yet it can be productive to examine two writers who are not contemporaries, where there is no clear influence, and who seem to have little in common, in order to see how far they illuminate one another.

Intersections

Some links suggest themselves straight away: a taste for the grotesque, a tendency to think in oppositional terms, an interest in the overreacher. Both were drawn to landscapes with figures, although Browning, asked if he cared for Nature, replied: "Yes, a great deal, but for human beings a

---

[4] Robert Browning, "Bishop Blougram's Apology", in *The Poems*, ed. by John Pettigrew, suppl. by Thomas J. Collins, 2 vols (Harmondsworth: Penguin, 1981), I, 642 (l. 996).

great deal more".[5] Tolkien – Greener than Browning – would have been less definite. Yet Tolkien's landscapes look back to Browning's. The nightmarish backcloth of "Childe Roland", for instance, prefigures Tolkien's Mordor – a land ravaged by a primitive industrialism.

Their moral perspectives overlapped. Both thought that the greatest wrongs spring from the urge to possess, coerce, and dominate others. To *use* another human being for one's own selfish ends is the ultimate sin, because it involves arrogating to oneself a God-like role. (Our tendency, nowadays, to castigate those who *abuse* others – as if *using* others is somehow acceptable – would have struck them as odd.) The characters in Browning who are witheringly criticised are the calculating, hypocritical, subtle manipulators, who lack all respect for others: the Duke in "My Last Duchess" is typical. Tolkien's take is similar: Sauron, the Lord of the Rings himself, being the grand example.

Two heroic romances

Biographically, they certainly had one thing in common. Each fell in love deeply once only, and the courses of their true loves did not run smooth. The popular image of Browning owes something to the film *The Barretts of Wimpole Street*, in which a Victorian St George rescues a sickly Elizabeth Barrett from the dragon's lair of her tyrannical father. Their courtship correspondence, before their secret marriage and escape to Italy, is justly famous. Before Robert had even seen Elizabeth (he was thirty-two, she was thirty-eight) he wrote to her in his first letter: "I love your verses with all my heart, dear Miss Barrett ...

---

[5] Quoted in G. K. Chesterton, *Robert Browning*, new edn (London: Macmillan, 1930), p. 186.

and I love you too".[6] From his poetry it seems that Browning believed in love at first sight; in his life he believed in something stranger still.

Tolkien was sixteen and living in Birmingham when he fell in love with a fellow-lodger, Edith Bratt; she was nineteen. They too had to carry on their (chaste) courtship clandestinely, avoiding the eyes of their landlady and Tolkien's guardian, Father Francis Morgan, who later ruled that the relationship must cease until Tolkien turned twenty-one. For three years they were not even allowed to correspond. At midnight on his twenty-first birthday he wrote to her to resume their relationship only to discover that she had become engaged to someone else; she had assumed that he had lost interest. She was persuaded to break off that engagement, convert to Catholicism, and three years later, as Tolkien prepared to embark for France with his regiment, they married.

Neither marriage was without its problems, but both relationships were sound. On Elizabeth's death at only fifty-five in 1861, Browning was devastated, and devoted himself to bringing up their only son, Pen; although gregarious, and capable of deep friendships with men and women, he stayed faithful to Elizabeth's memory, avoiding romantic entanglements and refusing a marriage offer from Louisa, Lady Ashburton. He died at seventy-seven, having been a widower for twenty-eight years and, unable to be buried in Elizabeth's tomb, was interred near Chaucer in Poets' Corner, Westminster Abbey. The Tolkiens' marriage lasted fifty-five years until Edith died in 1971 aged eighty-two. Tolkien, disconsolate, died two years later. On their tomb were inscribed the names of the

---

[6] *Robert Browning and Elizabeth Barrett: The Courtship Correspondence, 1845-1846: A Selection*, ed. by Daniel Karlin, (Oxford: Clarendon Press, 1989), p. 1.

two great lovers from *The Silmarillion* – Lúthien (immortal Elf-woman), and Beren (mortal man).

The comprehensiveness of Browning and Tolkien

One quality they shared as writers which partly explains their appeal is their voluminousness – indeed, their seeming comprehensiveness. Both were indefatigable writers. Both writing careers spanned fifty-six years. Browning's phrase, "The petty done, the undone vast"[7] applies to neither, while the word "prolific" does not do them justice. Browning wrote more than any other major English poet. Apart from his many letters and four prose works, Browning's output includes ten plays, three translations, thirteen long poems and eleven collections of shorter poems. The shorter poems add up to 325 individual items. "Shorter" is a little misleading: "Mr Sludge, 'The Medium'" weighs in at 1,525 lines. His longest poem, *The Ring and the Book*, is twice as long as *Paradise Lost*. And these are just the versions that survived. Browning, unlike Tolkien, destroyed all his drafts (and many finished poems).

The bibliography of Tolkien's published writings currently stands at 163 items. A number of works have still to be published. His translation of *Beowulf* has yet to appear. In fact, his posthumous writings outweigh those published in his lifetime. The compendious *History of Middle-earth*, edited by his third son Christopher, brings together excerpts from the many drafts of his evolving *legendarium*, of which *The Silmarillion* and *The Lord of the*

---

[7] Robert Browning, "The Last Ride Together", in *The Poems*, I, 609 (l. 53).

Rings are but parts; in twelve volumes, plus index, it runs to some 5,400 pages.

Browning and Tolkien: Their reputations and readers

Recognition came late to both. Browning, obviously, was never going to be a bestseller like Dickens. He was a poet, not a serial novelist, and he was writing at a time when the novel was rapidly becoming the dominant literary form. For many years Browning lived in the poetic shadow of his wife, Elizabeth Barrett Browning, who so nearly became Poet Laureate instead of Tennyson on Wordsworth's death. His attempts to write for the stage were conspicuous failures. That was partly to do with his choice of subject. *The Return of the Druses*, his play about an obscure medieval Lebanese religious sect, was never going to pull in the crowds. But it also had something to do with the fact that writing dramatic poetry and writing poetic dramas are not the same thing. Then there is *Sordello* – his 6,000-line narrative poem, about a minor thirteenth-century Italian troubadour, and a candidate for the most difficult poem in the English language – which blighted his reputation (and sales) for the next quarter of a century. Anecdotes about readers' bafflement are legion. Douglas Jerrold, recovering from brain fever, was given it as a present and found he could not make sense of it: "My God! I'm an idiot. My health is restored, but my mind's gone. I can't understand two consecutive lines of an English poem". Jane Welsh Carlyle claimed that by the end of the poem she still did not know whether Sordello was a man, a city or a book. Tennyson quoted the first line ("Who will, may hear Sordello's story told") and the last ("Who would has heard Sordello's story told") and said that they were the only two lines he could understand and both of them were false as far as he could tell. Ezra Pound wrote: "I began to get it on about the sixth reading". Browning's own comment when asked what it meant is apocryphal, but too good to omit: "Once there were two beings who knew what it meant – God and myself. Now God only knows what it means".[8] Browning was impatient with those who complained that his poetry was difficult. Ruskin wrote a letter to Browning full of questions about his poem "Popularity", which ends with the line: "What porridge had John Keats?" He complained: "I don't understand at all!!!!!!!!" Replying to Ruskin, Browning was clearly exasperated: "Do you think poetry was ever generally understood – or can be? Is the business of it to tell people what they know already...? A poet's affair is with God, to whom he is accountable ... Do you believe people understand *Hamlet*?"[9]

Gradually, however, Browning began to be revered as a sage with profound answers to life's big questions. Two signs of his newly-found cult status were the establishment of the Browning Society in 1881, and the start of a stream of publications about his writings. Quite a few writers have the accolade of societies formed to discuss their books, but rarely does it happen in their lifetime. Yet that is what happened to Browning: the Society even had branches in America and Japan. Books started to appear with titles such as *The Browning Cyclopaedia: A Guide to the Study of the Works of Robert Browning, With Copious Explanatory Notes*

---

[8] These anecdotes exist in variant forms: inevitably, perhaps, they tend to alter in the retelling. Most of them can be found in Philip Drew, *The Poetry of Browning: A Critical Introduction* (London: Methuen, 1970), pp. 70-74.
[9] The two letters are reprinted in John Woolford and Daniel Karlin, *Robert Browning* (London: Longman, 1996), pp. 252-59.

and References on all Difficult Passages.[10] His difficulty began to be part of his attraction.

As did his capaciousness. Like Shakespeare, Dickens, and the Beatles, Browning wrote about everything – art, religion, history, politics, society, philosophy, science, people ... He created a memorable gallery of *Men and Women*, historical and fictional; there are alchemists and con artists, doctors and dukes, lawyers and lunatics, monks and murderers, painters and poets, popes and politicians, rat-catchers and revolutionaries, saints and scholars, and many ordinary people. Just reading the titles of his poems conveys a sense of his range: *Pacchiarotto, and How He Worked in Distemper*; *Red Cotton Night-Cap Country*; *Prince Hohenstiel-Schwangau*; "Through the Metidja to Abd-el-Kadr"; "Rabbi Ben Ezra"; *"Dîs Aliter Visum, or, Le Byron de Nos Jours"*; "Ivàn Ivànovich".

All human life is there. That is not an obvious phrase to apply to Tolkien. Not because, as some have claimed, he ignores whole swathes of human experience, but because he goes beyond the human in order to represent it more truly. He created a whole mythology, an entire universe with its cosmogony, geography, geology, flora and fauna, and its various races, cultures, histories and languages. Dumas *père* is said to have remarked that, after God, Shakespeare created most.[11] That is a fair observation, for Shakespeare's linguistic inventiveness is unrivalled –

---

[10] Edward Berdoe, *The Browning Cyclopaedia: A Guide to the Study of the Works of Robert Browning, With Copious Explanatory Notes and References on all Difficult Passages* (London: Allen and Unwin, 1891).

[11] Cited by Jonathan Bate in his "General Introduction" to William Shakespeare, *Complete Works* [The RSC Shakespeare], ed. by Jonathan Bate and Eric Rasmussen (Basingstoke: Macmillan, 2007), p. 8.

though, at 40,000 words, Browning (who was given to *reading* dictionaries) had twice Shakespeare's vocabulary. But what would Dumas have made of Tolkien's creativity? Richard Hughes, previewing *The Lord of the Rings*, commented: "one can't praise the book by comparisons – there is nothing to compare it with".[12] As for Tolkien's vocabulary, or rather, *vocabularies*: the invented languages of Tolkien's world are but one of the features which help to make that world utterly real.

It is now commonplace to refer to the Tolkien industry. His much-translated books are worldwide bestsellers. What was a cult in the 1960s is now an international cultural phenomenon, only in part due to Jackson's film. The claim that *The Lord of the Rings* is *the* book of the twentieth century is not absurd: its sales and library borrowing figures and its continual topping of readers' polls underline his widespread appeal. He too saw a society founded to discuss his work, and scholarly studies of Tolkien show no sign of abating.

"Action in character": Browning's dramatic aesthetic

A recognition that we are all imperfect beings in an imperfect world is at the heart of the artistic credos of Browning and Tolkien. Poets are makers: the Greek *poiētēs* means "maker". For Browning "God is the [only] perfect poet":[13] first, because subjective perception and objective truth are at one in God – there can be no discrepancy

---

[12] Words quoted on the dust jacket of the first edition, and reprinted in Wayne G. Hammond and Christina Scull, "*The Lord of the Rings*": *A Reader's Companion* (London: HarperCollins, 2005), p. lii.

[13] Robert Browning, *Paracelsus*, II ("Paracelsus Attains"), in *The Poems*, I, 73 (l. 648).

between them – and second, because what God imagines *is* – not merely in conception but in reality. He makes, or *creates*, something – everything – out of nothing. God created man in his own image: he "imagined" man, and man thereby came into being.

Both Browning and Tolkien accepted that they were not true creators, but for different reasons. For Browning, human making is inevitably imperfect, finite. There is a disjunction, a hermeneutic lacuna between our subjective human perceptions and how things really are. We are part of the world we seek to understand. We cannot stand outside it. We cannot bypass our consciousness, and our consciousness is necessarily limited. We are like Hamlet in Shakespeare's play: he can never understand the meaning of the events in which he is caught up, not being the author of that play, being but a character, albeit the Prince of Denmark. This presented Browning with a seemingly insuperable problem. He wanted to be both Hamlet *and* Shakespeare, to understand reality from the inside and the outside, subjectively and objectively. But only God can do that. Browning's solution was the dramatic monologue (a poem in which a character other than the poet speaks to one or more – usually silent – listeners). He would explore the world around him from as many angles as possible. Browning's greatness as a poet springs from his mastery of that form.

That did not prevent him from admiring those poets (including his wife) who had the confidence to express their subjective vision, but his preferred poetic method, which he developed into a sophisticated aesthetic, was different. In a letter to Elizabeth Barrett he wrote: "… you *do* what I always wanted, hoped to do … You speak out, *you*, – I only make men & women speak – give you truth broken into prismatic hues, and fear the pure white light, even if it is in me …"[14]

In another letter he is clearer still: "I never have begun, even, what I hope I was born to begin and end, – 'R.B. a poem'".[15] In short, Browning eschews the lyrical in favour of the dramatic – a more tentative, exploratory, relative form. The result is an attempt at objectivity through endless subjectivities: what the French critic Charles Du Bos referred to as *l'introspection d'autrui* ("the introspection of another person").[16] One thinks of the late Paul Ricoeur's *Soi-même comme un autre*.[17]

"Mythopoeia": Tolkien's theory of fantasy

Tolkien's phrase for the constructing of his mythology was *sub-creation*, the making of worlds out of words. The key essay, setting out his Christian aesthetic, is "On Fairy-Stories", the second paragraph of which begins thus:

> The realm of fairy-story is wide and deep and high and filled with many things: all manner of beasts and birds are found there; shoreless seas and stars uncounted; beauty that is an enchantment,

---

[14] Robert Browning and Elizabeth Barrett: *The Courtship Correspondence, 1845-1846*, p. 5.
[15] Robert Browning and Elizabeth Barrett: *The Courtship Correspondence, 1845-1846*, p. 15.
[16] Quoted by J. Hillis Miller in "Trollope's Thackeray", *Nineteenth-Century Fiction*, 37. 3 [Special Issue: *Anthony Trollope, 1882-1982*] (December, 1982), 350-57 (p. 356).
[17] Paul Ricoeur, *Oneself as Another*, trans. by Kathleen Blamey (Chicago: University of Chicago Press, 1992).

> and an ever-present peril; both joy and sorrow as sharp as swords.[18]

Arguing against the view of mythology as a "disease of language" ("You might as well say that thinking is a disease of the mind"), he insists that "the association of children and fairy-stories is an accident of our domestic history".[19] Now stories, whether histories or myths, "are both ultimately of the same stuff".[20] For narrative, as Frederic Jameson has argued, is the central function of the human mind.[21] We think in stories. We learn and understand through stories. We communicate through stories. We all need good stories well told. But they are immensely powerful: "the invention of the adjective: no spell of incantation in Faërie is more potent", observes Tolkien. "Small wonder that *spell* means both a story told [as in 'gospel'], and a formula of power over living men".[22] And for the writer of fantasy everything depends on what Tolkien calls "the inner consistency of reality".[23] Such a story-teller

> makes a Secondary World which your mind can enter. Inside it, what he relates is "true": it accords with the laws of that world. You therefore believe it, while you are, as it were, inside. The moment disbelief arises, the spell is broken; the magic, or rather art, has

---

[18] "On Fairy-Stories", p. 3.
[19] "On Fairy-Stories", pp. 22, 34.
[20] "On Fairy-Stories", p. 30.
[21] Fredric Jameson, *The Political Unconscious: Narrative as a Socially Symbolic Act* (Ithaca, NY: Cornell University Press, 1981), p. 13.
[22] "On Fairy-Stories", p. 31.
[23] "On Fairy-Stories", p. 47.

failed. You are then out in the Primary World again, looking at the little abortive Secondary World from outside.[24]

(The "inside/outside" distinction should be familiar from Browning.) Fantasy is "not a lower but a higher form of Art, indeed the most nearly pure form, and so ... the most potent".[25] But "Fantasy has also an essential drawback: it is difficult to achieve":

> Anyone inheriting the fantastic device of human language can say *the green sun*. Many can then imagine or picture it. But that it not enough .... To make a Secondary World inside which the green sun will be credible ... require[s] labour and thought ...[26]

Fantasy, "founded upon the hard recognition that things are so in the world ... on a recognition of fact, but not a slavery to it", offers three things: "Recovery, Escape, Consolation, all things of which children have, as a rule, less need than older people"[27]

First, recovery, which Tolkien defines as a

> regaining of a clear view ... "seeing things as we are (or were) meant to see them" – as things apart from ourselves. We need, in any case, to clean our windows; so that the things seen clearly may be freed from the drab blur of triteness or familiarity – from possessiveness.[28]

---

[24] "On Fairy-Stories", p. 37.
[25] "On Fairy-Stories", p. 48.
[26] "On Fairy-Stories", p. 49.
[27] "On Fairy-Stories", pp. 55, 46.
[28] "On Fairy-Stories", pp. 57-58.

So one of its functions is to defamiliarise, to help us see reality afresh, in a new light, better to appreciate it. This is the doctrine of Browning's Fra Lippo Lippi, the fifteenth-century Florentine painter, who insisted that

> we're made so that we love
> First when we see them painted, things we have passed
> Perhaps a hundred times nor cared to see;
> And so they are better, painted – better to us,
> Which is the same thing. Art was given for that;
> God uses us to help each other so,
> Lending our minds out.[29]

Second, escape. Tolkien was scornful of those critics who dismissed "escapist literature": "they are confusing … the Escape of the Prisoner with the Flight of the Deserter".[30] This, too, Tolkien defamiliarises, particularly "the oldest and deepest desire, the Great Escape: the Escape from Death"[31] (a notion to which I shall return below).

Third, there is the consolation of the unlooked for "happy Ending … the sudden joyous 'turn' … giving a fleeting glimpse of Joy, Joy beyond the walls of the world, poignant as grief".[32] Tolkien ends the essay by stating that the writer of fantasy "may actually assist in the effoliation and multiple enrichment of creation", for: "Literature

---

[29] Robert Browning, "Fra Lippo Lippi", in *The Poems*, I, 547 (ll. 300-06).
[30] "On Fairy-Stories", p. 61.
[31] "On Fairy-Stories", p. 68.
[32] "On Fairy-Stories", pp. 68-69.

works *from mind to mind* and is thus more progenitive" (my emphasis).[33]

The same point is made in his poem "Mythopoeia", his defence of myth-making.[34] This starts by asserting that all language is an invention about reality. It is not in itself true: it is merely a way of understanding the world around us. Here is Tolkien as structuralist:

> You look at trees and label them just so,
> (for trees are "trees", and growing is "to grow") ...
> a star's a star, some matter in a ball
> compelled to courses mathematical ...[35]

But:

> ... trees are not "trees", until so named and seen –
> and never were so named, till those had been
> who speech's involuted breath unfurled,
> faint echo and dim picture of the world ...
> digging the foreknown from experience
> and panning the vein of spirit out of sense.[36]

There is nothing "true" about "tree": it is just a word invented, attached to that phenomenon. Until someone

---

[33] "On Fairy-Stories", pp. 73, 78.
[34] J. R. R. Tolkien, "Mythopoeia", in *Tree and Leaf*, new edn (London: HarperCollins, 2001), pp. 83-90.
[35] "Mythopoeia", p. 85 (ll. 1-2, 5-6).
[36] "Mythopoeia", p. 86 (ll. 29-32, 39-40).

came up with that name it was not a tree at all. The same with the word "star". What is it, really? A ball of matter moving on a mathematical course? But that is just how we see it. We are inventing our own terms, or accepting someone else's terms, about such things. Now (the argument runs), just as language is an invention about things, so myths or stories are inventions about truth. But that does not make them false:

> The heart of man is not compound of lies,
>
> but draws some wisdom from the only Wise,
>
> and still recalls him. Though now long estranged,
>
> man is not wholly lost nor wholly changed.
>
> Dis-graced he may be, yet is not dethroned,
>
> and keeps the rags of lordship once he owned …
>
> man, sub-creator, the refracted light
>
> through whom is splintered from a single White
>
> to many hues, and endlessly combined
>
> in living shapes that move *from mind to mind*.[37]

In other words: we have come from God and the myths we make, though not error-free, will be "splintered" fragments (Tennyson's "broken lights"[38]) of the original, white light of God's Truth – words from the Word. These lines are strikingly reminiscent of the words Browning used in the letter to Elizabeth Barrett quoted earlier (on pp. 11-12): "You speak out, *you*, – I only make men and women speak – give you truth broken into prismatic hues, and fear the

---

[37] "Mythopoeia", p. 87 (ll. 53-58, 61-64) (my emphasis again).
[38] Alfred Tennyson, in the "Prologue" (or "Introductory stanzas") to *Tennyson: In Memoriam*, ed. by Susan Shatto and Marion Shaw (Oxford: Clarendon Press, 1982), p. 37 (l. 19).

pure white light, even if it is in me". The metaphor, again, is that of "splintered" or "refracted light". So sub-creation is akin to the splitting and recombining of the original light to form the "living shapes that move from mind to mind". It is a metaphor not simply for artistic inspiration (sacred or profane), but for literary communication from writer to writer, from writer to reader, *from mind to mind*. And it is a rich metaphor. The word "mind" is traceable back as far as the inferred Indo-European **men*, "think". Nothing is more mysterious than thinking or feeling – the intangible, non-material processes of consciousness. Consider this description of the Arkenstone in *The Hobbit*:

> it was tinged with a flickering sparkle of many colours at the surface, reflected and splintered from the wavering light of [Bilbo's] torch … The great jewel shone before his feet of its own inner light, and yet, cut and fashioned by the dwarves … it took all light that fell upon it and changed it into ten thousand sparks of white radiance shot with glints of the rainbow.[39]

That is one way of conceptualising the electro-chemical process of so many neurons firing in the human brain. But however the rainbow is woven or unwoven – theologically, artistically, scientifically – it produces a sense of wonder in the human mind at such "multiple enrichment of creation".

Death as theme

Fascinated as Browning and Tolkien were by creativity – and creative artists abound in the works of both – there is another theme which looms large in Browning and

---

[39] J. R. R. Tolkien, *The Hobbit, or, There and Back Again*, 4th edn (London: HarperCollins, 1995), p. 213.

dominates in Tolkien, and that is death. Of course, all literature is about death "in the end". The urge to make art, to write, is a staving off, an attempt to attain a surrogate immortality, a bid to escape. Here is Larkin, sounding rather like one of Tolkien's elves:

> I write poems to preserve things I have seen/thought/felt ... both for myself and for others, though I feel that my prime responsibility is to the experience itself, which I am trying to keep from oblivion for its own sake. Why I should do this I have no idea, but I think the impulse to preserve lies at the bottom of all art.[40]

But while the death *topos* is ubiquitous in art, not all writers are obsessed by it to the same degree. Webster was not alone in being much possessed by it: so too were Dante, Donne, Milton, Keats, Tennyson, Beckett and Larkin. But neither Browning nor Tolkien is usually thought of in such terms. Browning is supposed to be the great Victorian optimist, and more major characters die in *Bleak House* than in *The Lord of the Rings*. Still, their writings are saturated with death and, in Tolkien's case, with the desire for deathlessness.

Death in Browning

Death in Browning is too vast a topic to begin to do justice to here. His poems are full of murders, suicides, death-bed scenes, dying confessions, and remorseful bereavements. Here is the speaker of his poem "A Toccata of Galuppi's" in meditative mode:

---

[40] Philip Larkin, "Statement", in *Required Writing: Miscellaneous Pieces, 1955-1982* (London: Faber and Faber, 1983), p. 79.

> "Dust and ashes, dead and done with, Venice spent what Venice
> earned.
> The soul, doubtless, is immortal – where a soul can be discerned …
>
> "As for Venice and her people, merely born to bloom and drop,
> Here on earth they bore their fruitage, mirth and folly were the
> crop:
> What of soul was left, I wonder, when the kissing had to stop?
>
> "'Dust and ashes!' So you creak it, and I want the heart to scold.
> Dear dead women, with such hair, too – what's become of all the
> gold
> Used to hang and brush their bosoms? I feel chilly and grown old.[41]

Thus Browning.

Tolkien on death and deathlessness

Tolkien on death has yet to be adequately examined. This is surprising. Tolkien himself often stressed its centrality to *The Lord of the Rings*:

> The real theme for me is about something much more permanent and difficult: Death and Immortality …
>
> … [and] the hideous peril of confusing true "immortality" with limitless serial longevity. Freedom from Time, and clinging to

---

[41] Robert Browning, "A Toccata of Galuppi's", in *The Poems*, I, 552 (ll. 35-36, 40-45).

> Time ... The Elves call "death" the Gift of God (to Men). Their temptation is different: towards a fainéant melancholy, burdened with Memory, leading to an attempt to halt Time.[42]

Tolkien's earliest tales, which date from the First World War, are all suffused with death. While Brooke, Sassoon, Owen, and Graves were writing their war poetry, Tolkien was embarking on an alternative project. As for the modernists: the luxury of detached experimentation that Yeats, Eliot, and Joyce enjoyed was not available to him. Tolkien was not meditating on the problem of suffering: he was caught up in it. Fortunately (for him and us) he escaped fairly early: diagnosed with trench fever, he was invalided home. During the Second World War, while writing *The Lord of the Rings* and carrying out his duties as an air-raid warden, his chief concern was for the welfare of his son Christopher who was serving in the RAF; that war, too, made its mark on his work.

The essential *donnée* of *The Lord of the Rings* is the Rings of Power themselves. In Tolkien's words: "The chief power (of all the rings alike) was the prevention or slowing of *decay* (i.e. "change" viewed as a regrettable thing), [and] the preservation of what is desired or loved ..."[43] The Rings fashioned by Sauron for "mortal men" are doubly escapist. They confer longevity *and* invisibility. But their anti-death powers are not what they seem. As Gandalf explains:

> "A mortal, Frodo, who keeps one of the Great Rings, does not die, but he does not grow or obtain more life, he merely continues, until

---
[42] *Letters of J. R. R. Tolkien*, pp. 246, 267.
[43] *Letters of J. R. R. Tolkien*, p. 152.

at last every minute is a weariness. And if he often uses the Ring to make himself invisible, he *fades*: he becomes in the end invisible permanently ..."[44]

Of supreme power is the One Ring, the ruling ring. Its evil purpose is to enable the Lord of the Rings to gain total dominance over Middle-earth. *The Lord of the Rings* is about the quest to destroy the One Ring, this ring that confers a spurious immortality. So at a profound level Tolkien's work confronts the reality of death and what he calls the "primordial" and uniquely human wish to escape from it.

But death is regarded ambivalently in Tolkien. One thing is plain: "immortality" is not to be confused "with limitless serial longevity". Galadriel and Elrond are not Nazgûl. This ambivalence runs like a fault-line through *The Silmarillion* and *The Lord of the Rings*, for the relations of, and the differences between, Elves and Men are central to both texts. Consider this statement from "On Fairy-Stories":

> The human stories of the elves are doubtless full of the Escape from Deathlessness. But our stories cannot be expected always to rise above our common level ... Few lessons are taught more clearly than the burden of that kind of immortality, or rather endless serial living, to which the "fugitive" would fly.[45]

The first sentence trips the reader up nicely. Tolkien is referring to the stories that "immortal" Elves write about humans. This is a technique he perfected in *The Lord of the*

---

[44] J. R. R. Tolkien, *The Lord of the Rings*, corrected 50th anniversary edn (London: HarperCollins, 2005), p. 47.
[45] "On Fairy-Stories", p. 68.

Rings: as if there were out there, somewhere, a stock of elvish tales, and if only we could get hold of them, well, that is what we would find. Thus Tolkien makes fantasy real. "Our" stories about Elves, however, written by us humans from our mortal perspective, are different. Wanting to escape from death, we hanker after immortality, yet the immortality of which we dream (such is the paucity of our imagination) sometimes amounts to mere "endless serial living". But the Elves dream of escaping from their burden of immortality by weaving stories of – death and dying! The wrong-footing reversal in Tolkien's off-hand, matter-of-fact comment ("doubtless") is deft.

Courage

But *how* should mortals face death? The answer that Browning and Tolkien both give is: with courage. The etymology of *courage* is from the Latin *cor*, "heart"; to encourage someone (in Italian: *coraggio!*) is to tell that person to take heart. Words of encouragement are words of comfort, and the word "comfort" means "strengthen" from the Latin *fortis*, strength. Courage, or fortitude, is one of the four cardinal virtues. Which is the most important of these virtues (courage, justice, prudence, and temperance)? To put the question another way: in your obituary which term would you rather have applied to you?

Browning and Tolkien, without doubt, would have said courage. Courage is a vital concept, and not to be confused with the bravado one meets in Icelandic sagas: in *The Saga of Grettir the Strong*, for instance, as he is dying of a spear-thrust, Atli remarks laconically: "They use broad spear-blades nowadays".[46]

Drawing upon a range of philosophers from Plato through Aristotle to St Thomas Aquinas, Paul Tillich, in his seminal study *The Courage to Be*, describes courage as "an affirmation which has in itself the character of 'in spite of'".[47] This emphasis is also to be found in that "early Northern literature" which Tolkien so admired. In "Beowulf: The Monsters and the Critics", Tolkien comments that this "theory of courage … is [that literature's] great contribution". He quotes from W. P. Ker's *The Dark Ages*: "The Northern Gods … are on the right side, though it is not the side that wins. The winning side is Chaos and Unreason … but the gods, who are defeated, think that defeat no refutation".[48] Might is not right. There is a marked similarity here with Browning, who took a perverse pleasure is staring defeat in the face. Many poets, especially Romantic poets, write nostalgically about the lost paradise of their childhood, or elegiacally about the death of a close friend. In his poem, "Prospice", which means "looking forward" (in both senses), Browning, typically, writes about the future, anticipating his own death. It begins, characteristically, with the words: "Fear death?" and goes on:

> I was ever a fighter, so – one fight more,
>
> > The best and the last!

---

[46] *The Saga of Grettir the Strong,* trans. by G.A. Hight, ed. by Peter Foote, new edn (London: Dent, 1972), p. 121.

[47] Paul Tillich, *The Courage to Be*, new edn (London: Collins, 1977), p. 16.

[48] J. R. R. Tolkien, "Beowulf: The Monsters and the Critics", in *The Monsters and the Critics, and Other Essays*, ed. by Christopher Tolkien, new edn (London: HarperCollins, 1997), pp. 20, 21.

> I would hate that death bandaged my eyes, and forbore,
>> And bade me creep past.
> No! let me taste the whole of it, fare like my peers
>> The heroes of old,
> Bear the brunt …[49]

So courage in the face of death is his adopted stance. Not a view which would win the approval of Philip Larkin who roundly asserted: "Courage is no good".[50]

What Tolkien admires is the spirit of determined "absolute resistance, perfect because without hope". This is true heroism, real courage. The cause is lost. Defeat and death are certain. But you fight on, against more than all the odds, knowing that you have lost, are losing, will lose. To quote Samuel Beckett: "you must go on, I can't go on, I'll go on".[51] This is no Dunkirk spirit, celebrating defeat as victory. It is the spirit encapsulated in the Old English poem "The Battle of Maldon", which relates how, in 991 during the reign of Æthelred, the Anglo-Saxon militia led by Byrhtnoð, Earl of Essex, were overwhelmed by the Viking invaders on the estuary of the Blackwater near Maldon, perhaps as a result of an over-confident (though noble) misjudgement by Byrhtnoð. In ceding passage to the Viking forces, perhaps out of a sense of fair play so that battle could be joined, Byrhtnoð "had blundered". The spirit of heroism is shown most clearly by an elderly retainer, Byrhtwold, who, in a famous speech, encourages the English warriors not to flee but to fight bravely on. His

---

[49] Robert Browning, "Prospice", in *The Poems*, I, 815 (ll. 12-18).
[50] Philip Larkin, "Aubade", in *Collected Poems*, ed. by Anthony Thwaite (London: Marvell Press, 1988), p. 209 (l. 37).
[51] Samuel Beckett, *The Beckett Trilogy*, new edn (London: Picador, 1979), p. 382.

speech begins with the two most famous lines in Old English poetry:

> Hige sceal þē heardra, heorte þē cēnre,
> mōd sceal þē māre, þē ūre mægen lȳtlað.

Translated, these read:

> Mind must be harder, heart must be bolder,
> Spirit must be greater, as our strength lessens.[52]

"Mind", "heart", and "spirit" are almost interchangeable here, in these stirring words that move from heart to heart, *from mind to mind*.

Byrhtwold continues:

> Here lies our lord in the dust, a hero
> All hewn down in battle. Ever will he mourn
> Who thinks to go now from this battlefield.
> I am an old man. Far from here I will not go,
> But I will die beside my lord,
> Lay down my life beside so dear a chief.[53]

Even though he must have felt that defeat might have been avoided and that their deaths were needless, he fought on, loyal to his lord. The same emphasis runs right through Tolkien's writings, from the mock-heroic *Farmer Giles of*

---

[52] "The Battle of Maldon", in *Sweet's Anglo-Saxon Reader in Prose and Verse*, ed. by Dorothy Whitelock, new edn (Oxford: Clarendon Press, 1970), p. 126 (ll. 312-13) (my translation).
[53] "The Battle of Maldon", (ll. 314-19) (my translation).

Ham: "But do you have to go to court and be a knight before you kill a dragon? Courage is all that is needed …"[54] Through *The Hobbit*:

> "Farewell, good thief," [Thorin] said. "I go now to the halls of waiting to sit beside my fathers, until the world is renewed … There is more in you of good than you know, child of the kindly West. Some courage and some wisdom, blended in measure … "[55]

To *The Lord of the Rings*, wherein Galadriel tells Frodo how "through ages of the world we have fought the long defeat".[56] For Tolkien this is the quintessential experience of "a mortal hemmed in a hostile world": "an ancient theme: that man, each man and all men, and all their works shall die. A theme no Christian need despise".[57] It is the theme of *Beowulf* itself which, Tolkien argues, was not an epic but an elegy about "the inevitable victory of death".[58] Beowulf "is a man, and that for him and for many is sufficient tragedy"; for "the wages of heroism is death".[59] Defeat, death in battle, are not sentimentalised by Tolkien. In his verse drama, "The Homecoming of Beorhtnoth: Beorhthelm's Son", a coda to "The Battle of Maldon", we read:

> Bitter taste has iron, and the bite of swords

---

[54] J. R. R. Tolkien, *Farmer Giles of Ham*, ed. by Christina Scull and Wayne G. Hammond, 50th anniversary edn, (London: HarperCollins, 1999), p. 30.
[55] *The Hobbit*, pp. 258-59.
[56] *The Lord of the Rings*, p. 357.
[57] "Beowulf: The Monsters and the Critic", pp. 22, 23.
[58] "Beowulf: The Monsters and the Critics", pp. 30, 31.
[59] "Beowulf: The Monsters and the Critics", pp. 18, 26.

> is cruel and cold, when you come to it.
> Then God guard you, if your glees falter!
> When your shield is shivered, between shame and death
> is hard choosing.[60]

The note struck, while not anti-heroic, is certainly anti-war.

Two quests

It is instructive to compare Browning's Childe Roland with Tolkien's Frodo Baggins. Both Browning's poem "Childe Roland to the Dark Tower Came" (which he described as "only a fantasy"[61]) and *The Lord of the Rings* are stories of quests, of course. Both "heroes" are seeking "the Dark Tower". Both narratives have a circularity about them: Tolkien's tale ends in the Shire, back where it started (twice), and the last line of Browning's poem is the same as its title.

"Childe Roland" is one of Browning's great monologues. But it is not dramatic: no one is listening to the speaker. Indeed, we must assume that Roland dies in the end, so quite how he tells his story retrospectively is something of a mystery. The psychology is in the grotesque landscape:

> A sudden little river crossed my path
>> As unexpected as a serpent comes …

---

[60] J. R. R. Tolkien, "The Homecoming of Beorhtnoth: Beorhthelm's Son", in *Tree and Leaf*, new edn (London: HarperCollins, 2001), p. 129.

[61] Quoted in William Clyde DeVane, *A Browning Handbook*, 2nd edn (New York: Appleton-Century-Crofts, 1955), p. 231.

>   how I feared
> To set my foot upon a dead man's cheek,
>   Each step, or feel the spear I thrust to seek
> For hollows, tangled in his hair or beard!
> – It may have been a water-rat I speared,
>   But, ugh! it sounded like a baby's shriek.[62]

Death is what is feared, plainly. But death may also be what is sought – feared *and* desired – as in Tolkien (the Elves envy Men their gift, the Men envy Elves theirs). "Childe Roland" is multivalent. Like *The Lord of the Rings*, this much-interpreted poem has been read and misread, allegorically and symbolically, by numerous critics. What does the Dark Tower represent? What are we to make of the ending? Does Childe Roland succeed in his quest, after so nearly failing? But, if so, what about his apparent death? The critics cannot agree. The idea for the poem came to Browning in a dream, and he wrote all 204 lines in just a day, on the 2nd January 1852, having written "Women and Roses" the day before; the next day he wrote "Love Among the Ruins", having taken a New Year's resolution to write a poem a day. (He failed to write anything on the 4th January.) Browning neither accepted nor repudiated most interpretations of the poem, admitting: "I had to write it … I did not know then what I meant beyond that, and I'm sure I don't know now. But I am very fond of it".[63] Later, when asked whether the meaning of the poem could be expressed in the biblical saying, "he that endureth to the

---

[62] Robert Browning, "Childe Roland to the Dark Tower Came", *The Poems*, I, 589 (ll. 109-10, 121-26).
[63] Quoted in a modern edition of Robert Browning's *Men and Women* (1855), ed. by Paul Turner (Oxford: Oxford University Press, 1972), p. 327.

end shall be saved" (Mark 13: 13), he is supposed to have replied "yes, just about that" – a remark that settles nothing, of course.[64] The late Paul Turner commented: "It is perhaps best not to attempt any detailed interpretation, but to regard the poem as a nightmare, expressing a mood of deep discouragement and self-distrust, plus determination to carry on".[65]

Frodo on Mount Doom is not quite the conundrum of "Childe Roland", but the climax to Tolkien's work does raise difficult questions. Did Frodo fail or succeed? Did the quest succeed because of, or in spite of, Frodo? Here is Tolkien:

> Frodo indeed "failed" as a hero, as conceived by simple minds: he did not endure to the end; he gave in, ratted ... [But] I do not think that Frodo's was a *moral* failure. At the last moment the pressure of the Ring would reach its maximum – impossible, I should have said, for any one to resist, certainly after long possession, months of increasing torment, and when starved and exhausted. Frodo had done what he could and spent himself completely (as an instrument of Providence) and had produced a situation in which the object of his quest could be achieved.[66]

Tolkien's reading finds corroboration in the text. When Frodo sets the Ring on his finger, he announces: "I do not choose now to do what I came to do"[67] Not, note, "I choose not to do", but *"I do not choose"*. Frodo is not wholly free to

---

[64] DeVane, p. 231. (He probably wanted to be rid of his questioner.)
[65] *Men and Women*, ed. by Turner, p. 328.
[66] *Letters of J. R. R. Tolkien*, p. 326.
[67] *The Lord of the Rings*, p. 945.

choose. Therefore his sin is not truly mortal, though later the quest will indeed claim his life: unable to remain on Middle-earth, he sets sail for the uttermost West and the Undying Lands.

The encouragement of Browning and Tolkien

Tolkien observed that "*The Lord of the Rings* is of course a fundamentally religious and Catholic work".[68] Browning's tastes were catholic, eclectic. Tolkien's appeal is catholic, universal. Both aspired to a Catholic comprehensiveness in their writings, producing plenitudinous worlds. One can imagine a Catholic writing the poetry of Browning; one cannot imagine a non-Catholic writing the works of Tolkien. I would argue that the wide and deep appeal of *The Lord of the Rings* is testimony to its "fundamentally religious" nature, and that it connects with its readers as powerfully as it does (all the more powerfully because subliminally) precisely because it confronts evil and suffering, defeat and death but, "dauntless", it offers what Tolkien called "Hope without guarantees".[69]

Clearly, at one level the literary projects of Browning and Tolkien could hardly be more different. But I have tried to adumbrate, tentatively, how at a profounder level, Browning through his psychologically acute dramatic poetry, and Tolkien through his extraordinary mythmaking and storytelling, are presenting us with perspectives on human experience that may not be so very dissimilar after all. I may be wrong. You may be unpersuaded. But, right or wrong, I would urge you to read them both.

---

[68] *Letters of J. R. R. Tolkien*, p. 172.
[69] *Letters of J. R. R. Tolkien*, p. 237.

Why? Harold Bloom offers one kind of justification for reading imaginative literature:

> Information is endlessly available to us; where shall wisdom be found? ... Reading well is one of the great pleasures that solitude can afford you, because it is, at least in my experience, the most healing of pleasures. It returns you to otherness ...[70]

John Carey's rationale for reading is similar; he argues compellingly that reading

> involves a kind of imaginative power different from anything required by other mental processes ... The imaginative power reading uniquely demands is clearly linked, psychologically, with a capacity for individual judgement and with the ability to empathize with other people. Without reading, these faculties may atrophy.[71]

I would suggest that reading Browning and Tolkien can, in vital ways, prevent such atrophy. And that is surely important. Ian McEwan, in a column published in *The Guardian* on the 13th September 2001, had this to say of the importance of the imagination:

> If the hijackers had been able to imagine themselves into the thoughts and feelings of the passengers, they would have been unable to proceed ... Imagining what it is like to be someone other

---

[70] Harold Bloom, *How to Read and Why* (London: Fourth Estate, 2000), p. 19.
[71] John Carey, "Why Read? A Polemical Introduction", in *Pure Pleasure: A Guide to the Twentieth Century's Most Enjoyable Books* (London: Faber and Faber, 2000), p. xi.

than yourself is at the core of our humanity. It is the essence of compassion and the beginning of morality.[72]

In their different ways, Browning and Tolkien offer imaginative ways of encountering otherness.

In the "Epilogue" to his last collection, *Asolando*, published on the day he died, Browning sets out his heroic ideal once more. It was a favourite of soldiers in the trenches of the First World War. The poem celebrates

> One who never turned his back but marched breast forward,
>   Never doubted clouds would break,
> Never dreamed, though right were worsted, wrong would triumph,
>   Held we fall to rise, are baffled to fight better,
>   Sleep to wake.[73]

There is no evidence that Tolkien read these lines, that there was any particular movement *from mind to mind*. But if he had read them, I think he would have approved. He would have felt encouraged. In *The Lord of the Rings*, introducing the tale of Beren and Lúthien to the hobbits, Aragorn observes: "It is a fair tale, though it is sad, as are all the tales of Middle-earth, and yet it may lift up your hearts".[74] Both Browning and Tolkien are, in this sense, encouraging writers.

---

[72] Ian McEwan's article, "Only Love and Then Oblivion", is available online at:
<http://www.ianmcewan.com/bib/articles/love-oblivion.html> [accessed 25 May 2007]. McEwan's argument has strong affinities with the artistic credos of Percy Bysshe Shelley and George Eliot.
[73] Robert Browning, "Epilogue", in *The Poems*, II, 931 (ll. 11-15).
[74] *The Lord of the Rings*, p. 191.